FIRST BIOGRAPHIES

W9-AOB-271

Thomas Jefferson

Cassie Mayer

Heinemann Library
Chicago, Illinois

© 2008 Heinemann Library
a division of Reed Elsevier Inc.
Chicago, Illinois

Customer Service **888-454-2279**

Visit our Web site at **www.heinemannlibrary.com**

All rights reserved. No part of this publication may be reproduced or transmitted in any form or by or by any means, electronic or mechanical, including photocopying, recording, taping, or any information storage and retrieval system, without permission in writing from the publisher.

Photo research by Tracy Cummins and Tracey Engel
Designed by Kimberly R. Miracle
Maps by Mapping Specialists, Ltd.
Printed and bound in China by South China Printing Company

10 09 08 07
10 9 8 7 6 5 4 3 2 1

10 Digit ISBN: 1-4034-9969-1 (hc)   1-4034-9978-0 (pb)
Library of Congress Cataloging-in-Publication Data
Mayer, Cassie.
  Thomas Jefferson / Cassie Mayer.
    p. cm. -- (First biographies)
  Includes bibliographical references and index.
  ISBN-13: 978-1-4034-9969-1 (hc)
  ISBN-13: 978-1-4034-9978-3 (pb)
 1. Jefferson, Thomas, 1743-1826--Juvenile literature. 2. Presidents--United States--Biography--Juvenile literature. I. Title.
  E332.79.M37 2008
  973.4'6092--dc22
  [B]
                                    2007009988

Acknowledgements
©Art Resource **p. 10** (NY/Erich Lessing); ©CORBIS/Bettmann **pp. 5, 14, 16, 19, 20**; ©Getty Images/Stock Montage **pp. 4, 13**; ©The Granger Collection **pp. 8, 11**; ©Library of Congress Prints and Photographs Division **p. 18**; ©National Archives **p. 15, 23**; ©Collection of New York Historical Society/1867.306 **p. 22**; ©The New York Public Library, Astor, Lenox and Tilden Foundations **p. 6** (Emmet Collection, Miriam and Ira D. Wallach Division of Art, Prints and Photographs); ©North Wind Picture Archives **pp. 9, 12**.

Cover photograph reproduced with permission of ©Getty Images/Stock Montage.
Back cover photograph reproduced with permission of ©CORBIS/Bettmann.

Every effort has been made to contact copyright holders of any material reproduces in this book. Any omissions will be rectified in subsequent printings if notice is given to the publisher.

Contents

Introduction

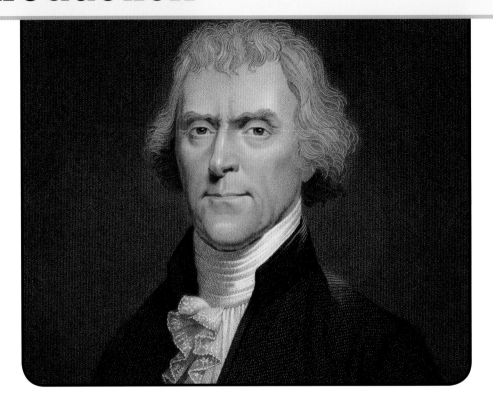

Thomas Jefferson was a president of the United States.

A president is the leader of a country.

Jefferson's home

Jefferson was born in 1743.
He lived in Virginia.

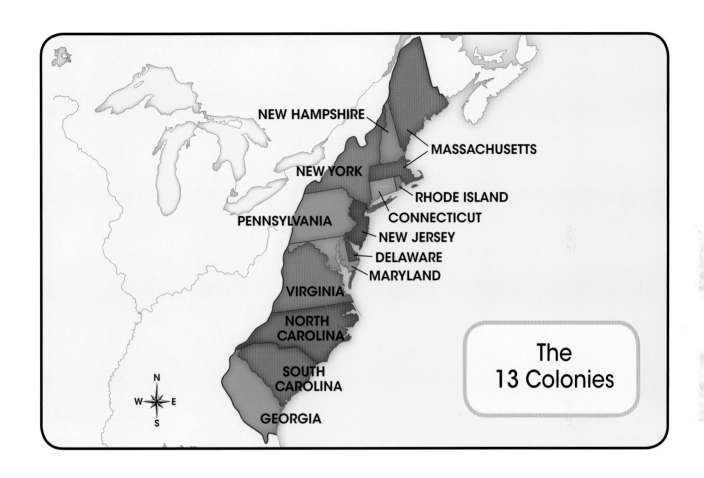

The United States was not a country yet.
It was called the American colonies.

The colonies were areas where people lived.

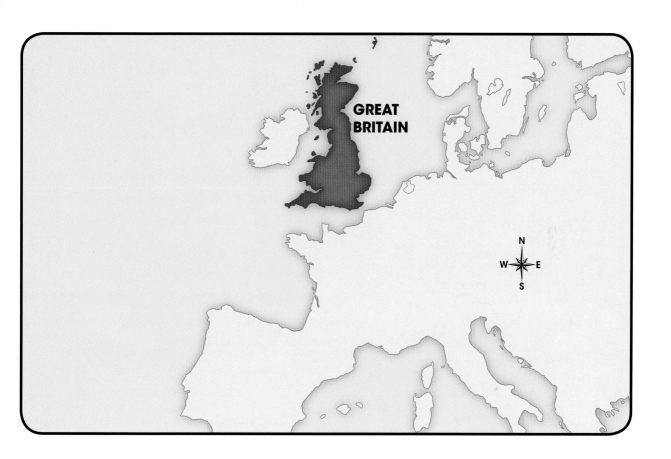

The colonies were led by Great Britain.

Early Life

Jefferson's books

When Jefferson was young, he loved to read.

When Jefferson grew up, he became
a great writer.

A New Country

In 1775, people in the colonies wanted to lead their own country.

A group of leaders met together.
They decided to write a paper.

The Declaration of Independence

They chose Jefferson to write the paper.

Declaration of Independence

The paper said why they wanted to lead their own country.

Revolutionary War

People in the colonies went to war with Great Britain. They fought to become a new country.

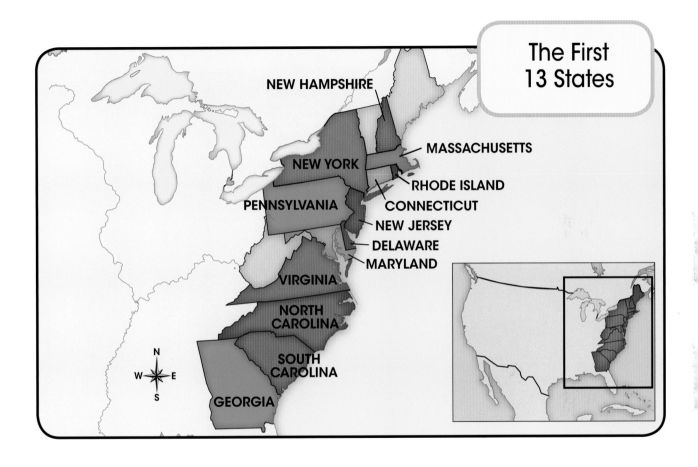

The First 13 States

NEW HAMPSHIRE
MASSACHUSETTS
NEW YORK
RHODE ISLAND
CONNECTICUT
PENNSYLVANIA
NEW JERSEY
DELAWARE
MARYLAND
VIRGINIA
NORTH CAROLINA
SOUTH CAROLINA
GEORGIA

They won the war. They became the United States of America.

A New President

Jefferson became president of the
United States in 1801.

He was the third president of the
United States.

The Louisiana Purchase

Jefferson bought land for the
United States in 1803.

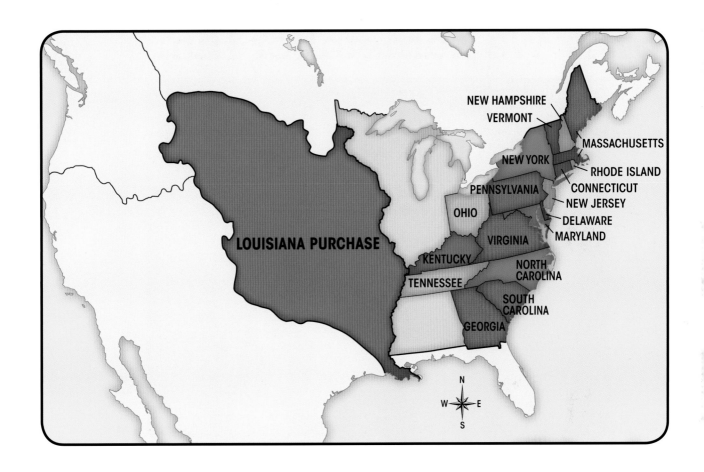

This was called the Louisiana Purchase.

Why We Remember Him

Thomas Jefferson thought about the future. He helped build the United States of America.

Picture Glossary

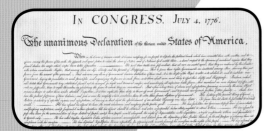

Declaration of Independence
a paper that said why colonists in North America wanted to lead their own country

Louisiana Purchase
an agreement where France gave land to the United States

Timeline

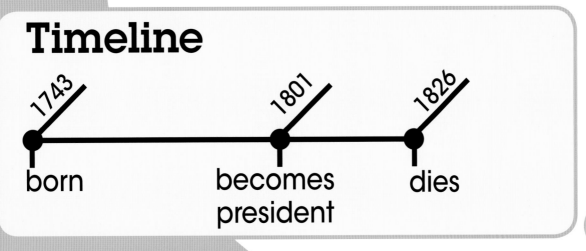

1743 — born

1801 — becomes president

1826 — dies

Index

Note to Parents and Teachers

This series introduces prominent historical figures, focusing on the significant events of each person's life and their impact on American society. Illustrations and primary sources are used to enhance students' understanding of the text.

The text has been carefully chosen with the advice of a literacy expert to enable beginning readers success while reading independently or with moderate support. An expert in the field of early childhood social studies curriculum was consulted to provide interesting and appropriate content.

You can support children's nonfiction literacy skills by helping students use the table of contents, headings, picture glossary, and index.